D1314333

Contents

Words to Know

beetle　　**lizard**　　**spider**

blue fish

blue frog

blue butterfly

blue beetle

blue bird

blue spider

blue crab

blue sea star

lizard with a
blue head

blue animals

Read More

Jenkins, Steve. *Living Color.* Boston: Houghton Mifflin, 2007.

Whitehouse, Patricia. *Colors We Eat: Purple and Blue Foods.* Chicago: Heinemann, 2004.

Web Sites

Animal Colors
<http://www.highlightskids.com/Science/Stories/SS1000_animalColors.asp>

Animal Printable Coloring Pages
http://thecoloringspot.com/animals-coloring-pages/

Index

Guided Reading Level: A
Guided Reading Leveling System is based on the guidelines recommended by Fountas and Pinnell.

Word Count: 24